FREE

Richard Barrett

Published by BLART BOOKS

www.blartmagazine.jimdo.com

ISBN 978-1-291-54497-8

AN UA

The Red Rec (Re-Run Channel)

Penniless Poetix

AN UA

Huge thanks to Phil Davenport for including AN UA in his language art anthology *The Dark Would* (2013) and for invaluable editorial suggestions and guidance during the composition period of the piece.

Running,

Alongside the train

He is running.

Possessive meaning a binary. So hence, I think, the speed of this train. ‘Disquiet’ is such a twee word whilst this place is so flat & why is that I wonder & is there an alternative … *It being only ownership that separates these feet from those*. Anyway, there’ll always be the sunburnt neck. Or the way the earth’s been shaped – hill-less. The flash convincing no one the sun is still out, rather, just spoiling the picture. One gets older and in that getting older is a poetry.

Who wants an originary poetry? Maybe an impulse time specific, which is to say ‘reactive’ which isn’t to say ‘reactionary’ of course. There is a dump-bin by the till full of disposable cameras. Okay. So now I’ll read the whole of the sign & coz it’s funny will laugh & you’re laughing. In regard to doctor and patient satisfaction remember ‘Waiting limited to 4 hours’. Change to be welcomed wherever it comes from. & Cliques form and cliques split up yes but me I see nothing bad about language in flux.

Maybe disturbing maybe. Or may be disturbing. I might take all the words within the ring this coffee cup has left
on this Ron Silliman poem and might make my own out of them. And you notice the friendliness and smiles have changed to serious looks as well now eh … ? But let’s not have that conversation just yet – . Still, impossible to keep from waiting. I mean waiting as an activity opposite to passive, i.e. an active activity: I’m sat here and waiting but in doing so really feel like I’m doing – um – something. Y’know? The text will come through eventually; causing the display to light-up which, from its place in the shirt pocket, will cause the face to light-up as well.

Which is to say all still to come. For expediency’s sake I mean taking the restrictions of the remit very much into account it's hard to think other than that the hand has been forced. To time-travelling, backwards. Wait and someone will soon flag-up the arbitrariness of the choice to focus on just that strata of the earth over every other strata. Asserting their authority and making expert statements of feelings and facilitating conversations. The sun is out I see. Yes. So shall we sit out? It'll be nice and when it gets too cold we can come back in. Okay.

[Running, alongside the train, a leopard is running.] But is the tube still running? The pulled grille means, just, well, that this entrance is closed – so let's cross. Nearly 4 years to the day with no booze. No, it was only 3. Now here I am & here's my can of Stella. You say 'This Cider's nice. Have a taste'. I do; and it is. But the days bear down now, so . . . oppressively. Meaning: exactly what? That isn't how people think or talk.

& my neck feels, now, not up to giving sufficient support. It was a late night last night. With words, *over-wrought this bit might be, sorry*, betraying … not at all actually, no. It didn't happen like that. Yes it did happen like that. And sweating, dripping, received us falling, and flung in shimmering arcs across the room (ha!). It would make sense to write I think. Pages and pages deleted though. Work submitted for consideration to be added to the archive of manuscripts they deleted. Who would do that? Well. I've been thinking about it.

& not just that. No. The assumption being of a non non-drinking situation picked up from several of the things said. An old strategy. But . . . seriously I mean – something seems to be being implied as under threat here. What? Under this, I'll just check the camera. Well, what colour was the sky the last time you travelled home by train in April; the start of the month say – 7ish? One can write or not write of course but – ultimately it feels kind of irrelevant which choice is made. Words taking one further from the truth. Which is bad. But I don't know what to do about it. Nor how to write.

Peterborough. Finally. Leaves on the tracks opposite seen through the seat gaps being a metaphor for this. With which they can defend themselves. Though only a temporary fault. It didn't miss. No, all he was interested in was the weather all around, everywhere, as far as the eye could see. Last night on the telly he remembered the weatherman had said something. But what, now, he just couldn't remember. But staying up late tonight with no work tomorrow would be cool I reckon. Staring at this computer screen writing - which feels like just the latest time when I'm doing something to distract myself from thinking about not doing the thing which I really should be doing. Et cetera. Managing down loss across the board. When I looked at the figures this morning I felt like crying.

Like another game of Scrabble online. My stats being not quite what they used to be I mean, like, only two months ago or something. All I can say is that I feel I can't do it so well now. Worse, they seem to be actively anti-truth. I feel embarrassed by this. I feel embarrassed, as well, by my embarrassment as I feel there's really nothing to be embarrassed about. Probably I should just send a message, yeah? But right now I couldn't even say why. The dominance, the authority, the expert status – the doctor is a liar. Which affects the binary system how? Does it affect the binary system? Should I live somewhere else? But I prefer during the afternoon for things to stay just nice and chilled I mean. We've had our good time of course. And again, soon.

That's true isn't it? I mean, if both those positions are beyond the strength of a local man or woman, no matter how strong they may be at any given moment, then they're fucked, right, basically. *But they can still try and make it to the peak* – . Calf and thigh muscles are strong I feel. Then - *my father linked his arm through mine and we raced back down to the sea* – er, when (?) . . . We didn't. We wasted time doing foolish shit just because we thought it might earn us a bit more fame. He confided. He confided. The seriousness with which this pronouncement was made indicating to me I was indeed intended to take it seriously. And would have to be observed to get the full picture. Putting my face, flush, against the ground the smell of grass and the earth then was intoxicating. Meaning, what the alcoholic had for breakfast? What was that? The list is being recited now and is within spitting distance still, thankfully, of the poem. And, as well, his undeveloped storyteller's instinct.

Wondering – . In fact I have been doing so for the last couple of days. But am irritated by coyness. Writing doesn't seem to make sense. Would only result in more disturbance of one kind or another when everything is geared, or at least should be geared at the moment, towards avoiding upset of just that variety. Yet the risk positions cannot be overlooked. Taking into account, too, the question of appropriate response: upon receipt of a message made up of those words, or similar – anyway, clear unambiguous words – . I'll just open some windows then; or leave the door open a bit, a bit. I think. Yes, thankfully the mood does always seem to pass. & I have learnt not to set too much store now by information gleaned from Facebook. Which maybe is something I should have learnt sooner? I am excited. This feels exciting. People are acting excited. And saying they're excited. I don't know if more or less excited than anyone else.

I don't know where this is. But I think I know where I want it to be. And with who. Honestly, if someone could take me there now I would never move from that place. And would think constantly of everyone else whose steps had ever passed over that place. And the jumpers they wore. And where they were going and who they were going back to and how much they loved them or thought they loved them or hoped that they loved them and I'd think of what they'd drink that evening and of what they'd eat too and I'd hope that they weren't snotty about TV and finally I'd think of just how many hard decisions they'd had to make to get them to that place. Because I can do that you know. Of course, it'd be a never-ending job. B u t. T h e n. W h a t. E l s e. W o u l d. I. B e. D o i n g. I n s t e a d?

Exactly. So shut down the Facebook tab. The uncalmness of mind, eyes flickering, exacerbated by the number of things going on on the one screen, middle, up, then down again. A blessed fatalism best embraced. Whilst considering a possible mis-diagnosis. Does an aching lower-back mean too vigorous a work-out at the gym or the start of a cold & how quickest would this problem be solved? Has your mind ever flitted back and forth in quite this way before? If pushed for an answer that answer would probably be – . Oh (!), every answer will differ. Anyway, it feels today like something got done. Yesterday was so very hot – *. An f romclo c k ing in To l u nch [then]*a s in f r om heav'n *he fell, from* [Scientifik M a n age men t] *fromf ro m f ro mfromfrom . . . to d ewyeve H e –* . 'npicked. Separated from fear and a nervous expectation of future unhappiness. Then, well, to be able to write that down. I hear laughing. At me? And the ridiculous importance I give to writing? Come home / And we'll talk shit to ya.

Because, ultimately, well, not 'ultimately', no (why 'ultimately?); immediately, rather.

Writing is no substitution for doing. Shirt-sleeves rolled-up in the alpha-male environment of the US 1970s creative-writing workshop, braces down, looped. Palpable sense of urgency. Can only be a prevarication or a repeated excuse for inaction. So if one wants something one should go get it? I want coffee. Cup stains on text-books working as some kind of pathway through language. Stepping stones to the twee (what I once believed the left-bank of a river was called). Coffee-cup stain constellation. A browny-yellow Olympic logo now covering pages 192-193 of Lenin's *What Is To Be Done?* Detracting from re-sale value. Anyway, I expect negligible, seeing as it only cost me in the first place a couple of quid. Some places are hilly right. Others aren't. Being no good with tastes. Being the refrain of – attempting to reacclimatise to – wherever. Right, ask me to describe this drink; how it tastes etc, and I just won't be able to I tell you. I'd say of course I can remember the old days I have a remarkably good memory. Likewise, I didn't invent coffee.

See the empty bottle of Actimel, the coins and the watch. Those mantelpiece whatnots. Imperative to leave; felt urgently. Returning though, shamefacedly, to the word. Institutionalised. As we know work can do that having seen with our own eyes the institutionalising effects upon some people that we like &, sorry to say, seen a warning there. Okay, so, yeah, I know now, today, it's questionable just how sensible that is. But what is the other person doing right now? Whoever that other person is. And what am I doing? What could I be doing? Well, there is different landscape. In the literal sense of the southern flatlands and northern hills . . . and the strictures of the remit – meaning deadlines. Meaning that sense of a chance missed (possibly). Just passed. But maybe that's a new development? So of course opportunities for travel. Train being a perennial whilst newer being the bus. The tube as a variant of the first. Bus journeys feeling somehow like betrayals. That by going to this place and I am I am consciously rejecting going to that other place.

Which would be better. Because of circumstance. Because of circumstance. Because of circumstance. Due to that place being where the other is. You see these 'doubts' now seem unreal; doubts flagged up only for drama. Certainly. Certainty returning certainly *I think* I mean guaranteed absolutely to return whenever and at whatever slight sign might be deemed appropriate. So there's writing *still*, & always. Geology being no substitute. Nor conversations on the same ('in m y ar e a,isth i s th e c li me, ist h is the soil, t urn e do v er c era mic t ile[ex-b athr o om]', Said then the lost Archangel; 'I' lls t ickw iththe gang of one;ca rv e a ho le in the r a in for yer'). And, really, only uncertainty as to why the subject proved so very fascinating for group-uscles of the past. My interest in the flat extending no further than land you needn't walk up or down but can instead just pass over – as calmly as you like & with as little energy expenditure. I absolutely would live there however though. Where aims meet limitation, enforced. Deleted. Which means – *annual this isn't, nor* – civil liberation for Dogs. [[Running, alongside the train, a leopard is running.]]

Seeking to travel back to where language came from. To convey something specifically British. Which I turn away from for lack of interest. Thinking, at the same time though, and post the conversation with him knowledgeable in outdoor wear, that my turning away is only possible due to them choosing not to. Choices are made and the primary one was to turn to a poetry fitting for the age & with all that that means. The carving out of a space therefore cannot be done Here.

In Manchester. Or cannot be done alone here in Manchester. Disguise, then, serious things as jokes. Hidden. This confidence fooling no one. A blip. In other words, the confidence of the forever under-confident. But must keep repeating that things will work out okay. Yes, repeat that. Diffusing via humour and with long-winded digressions. Believing truth best approached that way. But why this fetishisation of truth (if that's what it is) eh? Succeeding only in marking one out as some kind of – um – dinosaur or something? Subject matter dictating approach I think. I mean, if something is important and I care about it then, well, it's important to be truthful. It's only one tool among many – excusing likely exaggerations, sorry. One tool amongst . . . two. Or a couple. In other words, yep, two. & thereby the return of the binary which is beginning to resemble some kind of sad obsession now . . . there are only opposed positions, 2 of them. Here is not There. Nor Contentment Discontent. Nor Him, er, Her.

Valuable Facebook. This weekend a subject that's come up often. How important is location? I am somewhere and want to be somewhere else and so, then, in such circumstances as those I would say of unique significance – as an irritant. I want all locations to be one. The usual rules of space to apply no longer. Which, I suppose, means also would have the knock-on effect of fucking time right up as well. Like some child's toy exposed by Esther Rantzen as containing a potentially lethal metal spike. I spent so long on that message . . . was there a message? A kind of palate cleanser or rehearsal to avoid thinking about compromised authenticity – the impossibility of sustaining the illusion that

everything might still turn out alright. But it might. Sure. And I'll keep saying that. Expecting soon to experience the sensation of feeling I'm sitting somewhere other than where I really am sitting ie not here on this wooden stool which is a bit wobbly but on some two-seater sofa with my arse about one foot off the floor – you sink right back into it that much. The psychedelic essence of Salvia Divinorum. So where will trains, tubes and buses be then eh. Keeping us, I mean, not us as in me and one specific other, I mean us as in everyone that is to say anyone else with any other person else in touch. There'll still be there. Disembodied, colourful and blissful. I pulled back, wondering, from what seemed like nearly one hundred feet where I was. So where is this? The letter L is lost. And N. this will never be a yearly event.
But back to waiting. & what is more important I'm thinking, a belief in the validity of waiting as a worthwhile activity. Waiting is easy. I am a world champion at it (mis-typed as word. Coz what is this other than a text? This is not an experience. It isn't happening). But it is linked. I feel tense. And I can wait as long as I

can write. As, as has already been established writing is merely done due to anything better being absent. As well, regarding that relationship – . Which is to say, the relationship between what is now happening and what might be happening elsewhere – with one of those where's being here. The other being, else – okay. So what is happening then in every sense of happening. *Look at how these words appear on this screen – excesses of certain fleeting sensations.* & the similarity between waiting and writing. SMS messages are not importuning nowadays nor designed to elicit any negative emotion – . So how to think of that other than as a side-effect (happy) of a more grown-up grasp of the language game then? *Then that connection between writing better and living happier. . . ?* Over a certain amount of time has passed now which can range from years to much shorter periods such as hours, minutes or seconds. Imagine the location – . Next, imagine yourself there. What is the dominant emotion right now? Whatever, remember – it was A s u mmer'sda y: a n dth e s e t tingsunDrop pe dfro m t he z e n it h like a fall ings t a r. An d o nceit h ad . . . An dla u gh edth r ou gh t wiste d m ouths – andonc e itha d – we were sad it was over of course but very very glad we'd been around to see it happen.

Running, alongside the train, a leopard is running. I find the time lag very interesting. How writing can never be the thing coz of the delay involved. Which I'm using, incorrectly, as a synonym of disappointing. But consciously. To pre-empt any smart-arsery . . . *committing* smart-arsery. Oh yes then so this shit does bother me believe me. Sorry, of course you believe me – how could anyone doubt the 5 year old email thread which I didn't mean to bring-up sorry coz I know it isn't needed as you just have to say believe me and of course I do and . . . vice-versa. Me and you we say – fuck your bourgeois need for proof! Writing over the me. Behind, rather. And the you, I and us. Is passive-aggression? The person who writes. One gets older and in that getting older is a poetry. The question was regarding how to reopen that exchange then; and on that same level after so much time had passed. So how to do that? And by avoiding the hamfistedness of earlier attempts. Remember, time has passed. Kings X at just gone eleven. No, it doesn't all have to be pealing bells now of course . . . ! It is the humanity, most, that is interesting here. The swinging from anger to intellectual detachment to vulnerability. Humour. What is the relationship between doing and representation? And how does that relationship impact upon the imaginary one and the imaginary other? Are things that I ask myself, some of them; on the train, firstly.

Where the hills aren't and then, later, after that, where the hills are again. It gets said 'you will never leave this town'. That nexus of forces. Meeting, here, in the body in Manchester which is other, but at the same time, the root from which all else has grown. In the past. And going on. Forwards. Keeping us, I mean, not us as in me and one specific other, I mean us as in everyone that is to say anyone else with any other person else in touch. They'll still be there. Disembodied, colourful and blissful. With time present containing time past et cetera . . . we were

there . . . scoping the perimeter . . . round
Fairfield street . . . Age meaning something I
would have done easy way back then
becoming now, um, something requiring
tonnes and tonnes of research. I don't know
how R******* got in, no so I will ask her. The
ghost station. And the ex-flatmate. Anyway, a
certain amount of time has passed now –
maybe years, maybe – much shorter periods –
possibly hours, minutes or seconds. So then –
imagine the location – . Next, imagine yourself
there. I mean, imagine a dissatisfaction with
how things stand and a need to convert things
to something other? Some genetic male hang-
up perhaps? This is just a building. An old
building. And all we're doing is walking round
it. T his c r um my blitz trad, S hould b e,a n
d,   b yc o ncur ring signs,e re now,Cr e atedv
ast andr o und[t h e sed ust ypic t u res],th
ismass o f b lon dec urls, In the purlieus of
Heav'n – . And that is enough. And I will
remember this walk around this building 5
days from now. I will be reading accounts
online of what people found here. Pictures,
too. I will be looking at pictures too. And I
will see the picture of you stood in front of the

huge, painted, blue bird on the wall we took that day. I found a picture of you. Trying to find the picture of you. 'cause I'd probably take a picture of you. In front of the huge, painted, blue bird on the wall we took that day. And though that first thought is rarely correct it is always necessary (I believe absolutely and completely so) as we only arrive at our rightful place after first having been through – oh —— – any number of wrong places.

Or so I was told once. Thinking of transcendence and immanence and what separates the two. Or how many fucking counties keep Point A and Point B apart (which is hard when your geography's shit. Though it may be geography in general rather than just mine that I have the problem with. Geography is shit). Interpretation always mediated by context means not that interpretation should be given up on but that, rather, the limitations of method should be pushed foreground. To document the obsession. What sort of document is this, or obsession even? Or will it become? Wait and someone will soon flag-up the arbitrariness of the choice to focus on just that strata of the earth over every other strata. Okay, so, yeah, I know now, today, it's questionable just how sensible that is. But what is the other person doing right now? Whoever that other person is. And what am I doing? What could I be doing? Well, there is different landscape. In the literal sense of the southern flatlands and northern hills . . . and the strictures of the remit – meaning deadlines. Meaning that sense of a chance missed (possibly). Just passed. But maybe that's a new development? Starting out on this path my mental health was questioned regularly. Though what separates this from something a child could do is the exposition right, yeah? I mean, in theory, any 6 year old could do that but they couldn't talk about it the way you just have. Thanks are given. Thanks. And the question of if another drink is required can be seen formulating in the brain. Entering the surrounding air via the aperture of the mouth before going on to penetrate the other's ear. Putting my face then, flush, against the ground the smell of grass and the earth was intoxicating. Now things seem to happen in slow motion . . . How did I get here? This is not my part-time job. This is not my beautiful girlfriend. This is the house of my father with – . And – . A mother who's dead. Upset, the glass doesn't wobble. We watch the glass travel back to when language began. To convey something specifically British. Which I turn away from for lack of interest. And the liquid puddles around it on the table-top. The glass of Summer Fruits smoothie. The cup of funny smelling tea. Yes, I will have the same again please.

The Spirit of Man is a pub I go in. How can you have the same again? You can have it, first, walking round this ex-rail station and, second, writing about the walk later. In other words, yep, two. & thereby the return of the binary which is beginning to resemble some kind of sad obsession now . . . there are only opposed positions, 2 of them. Here is not There. Nor Contentment Discontent. Nor Him, er, Her. Which is what's happening here. I will try to be funny. The hope being to wow her with humour and by so doing disguise the essential ridiculousness of what I am suggesting. I would say the usual rules of space no longer apply. And I'll keep saying that. Expecting soon to experience the sensation of feeling I'm sitting somewhere other than where I really am sitting ie not here on this wooden stool which is a bit wobbly but on some two-seater sofa with my arse about one foot off the floor – you sink right back into it that much. The reprise tainted by the memory of what came after though. We dig back through numerous strata of the earth and yet find nothing that resembles God. Clearing the garden of broken ceramic bathroom tiles I wonder how language is transmitted and received. Which is beginning to resemble some kind of sad obsession now . . . Suffering the dehydration of early afternoon though today my receiver is down; instead I'm relentlessly hammering words out to appear before me, cold and unforgiving, on this computer screen. Thinking of deleting them. What is humour? Everything is qualified. No statement possible without the encumbrance of objection. I cannot say anything. And (sigh) all information is not online. Adorno counsels of the importance of seeing things from both inside and out, simultaneously – which is to say, of course, at once. And correct I think. Travelling down, Saturday coming, I am travelling first class. The first time that I have. That class not requested just a seat in the quiet carriage and here I've never seen such smug-looking, self-satisfied bastards in my whole life. I want to kill them all. Every one of them. Their absurd sense of entitlement.

But let's not have that conversation just yet – . Still, impossible to keep from waiting. Following a casual remark to the effect that the regard in which he's held surprises. The original partner disappeared. One rumour said to Texas. Following a casual remark – . Regarding the way the earth's been shaped – . My interest in the flat extending no further than land you needn't walk up or down but can instead just pass over – as calmly as you like & with as little energy expenditure. I absolutely would live there however though. *But don't think about that too much now* – instead, we responded with, limiting ourselves to just 3 or 4 lines, the first few things that we could think of . Which went on for about three weeks. Before the edit. And before the reading. To which, having given our apologies, we arrived about 3/4s of an hour late. We'd needed food, see. Those 'doubts' now seeming unreal; doubts flagged up only for drama. Certainly. Certainty returning certainly *I think* I mean guaranteed absolutely to return whenever and at whatever slight sign might be deemed appropriate. Okay, 'I will wait here then / until I grow a beard'. Lay on a spread out duvet on your living room floor, your flatmate away, the single-bed having been abandoned as we kept falling out of it, finally – we slept. You said, I like it when you don't shave. I said, but I look a mess when I don't shave. I was just that un*hairy*. Retrieving the poem from the carrier bag whilst the other guy was reading resulted in people wishing death upon me with their eyes. Sitting on the floor is cool. Or was cool. Or *is it cool?* I don't think I know what cool is now though . . . Okay, so look up then . . . A ndreadth y l o tin y once l e sti als ign, *a n y w a y* – it wa s a b igt ea-c h estf u c kero fad og. Which makes a change. The landscape being one factor amongst many influencing how you produce literature (ha!) Anyway, it all felt cool. Sitting there with you. With people.

Coming up to us sat there, on the floor. Asserting their authority and making expert statements of feelings and facilitating conversations. Avoiding the direct approach. Always. This confidence fooling no one. A blip. In other words the confidence of the forever unconfident. How when some people talk they talk as though they're a fucking customer satisfaction survey with all their agree/disagree strongly shit and that. And how bad that is as it dehumanises and is related to fascism. So one can write or not write then in circumstances like those of course but – ultimately it feels kind of irrelevant which choice is made. Words taking one further from the truth. But our talking round the houses, and the talking round the houses of others we know, being just our way, I mean how and who we all are, not any kind of conscious battling of anything . . . Anyway, couching language in ambiguity means anything received and understood as being something the other would rather not have heard can just be brushed away as a mistake - ! But . . . here comes Tom. And Andy. And Frances. And Allen now . . . Outside there is a city. Beyond it lies your home with, in another direction, mine. How did the earth become shaped like this? How did life *one* end up placed where it is whilst life *two* ended up placed somewhere altogether different? There are trains, buses, helicopters and tubes to help us overcome geography but can anything we do help us overcome money? *Look, I really want to know the answer to that . . . !* My sad obsession. My interest extending no further than – . My turning away – . My arse – . My mental health. And my part-time job . . . Your comment on Facebook seemed to suggest that a choice needed making there where I saw no choice necessary. Hence why I deleted it (which, okay, I feel daft about now, but) – why not have both? Why not have more than both? Have everything.

The tube is still running. The grille isn't pulled yet. Nor will it be pulled for a while. An hour or so, only, with no booze means . . . I'll be drinking soon. Red Stripe. Bought from the shop. Cans. 4 of them. You say 'I can't believe you've bought more'. I say 'you drink less now, yeah? Are you sure you don't want one?' Which is how people talk and think, prior to talking. Tuesday I will go to the gym. I am developing quite impressively pronounced muscles in my arms. Sweating heavily. Rushing, to hit Kings X before the last train leaves. Seriously. One can write or not write of course and as this is the C21st it's probably just easier to text. Feeling kind of irrelevant. We will part with, as we do, promises being made for August. Pages and pages deleted with, yet, still though, pages and pages sent. I checked last night – having stayed up late with no work in the morning – I copied and pasted onto Word the whole of that one message . . . Just the latest time doing something to distract myself from thinking about not doing the thing which I really should be doing (whatever that is). I counted the words. And . . . Back in my room in South Ealing, the walls bearing in so oppressively . . . I thought of you. And thought of the day that had just been. And thought of tomorrow. I will see you again soon. And comforted by the memory of how your body felt held close to mine I fell asleep.

Binary thinking, always. Erased from my Facebook page. Why is that I wonder? The preventative of the sunburnt neck, obviously, is sunscreen. Though no danger of sunburn today. Instead just scalding, minor, as I upset the table and coffee spills onto my thighs and the floor. A cheap way of passing the time will be journeying back and forth, an hour each way, to the hotel in Ealing. Will you come? I'd be able to dump my bag and change these jeans. They are disposable. Okay. Change to be welcomed wherever it comes from then – even the British Library foyer. Just round the corner from the Caledonian Road. An action shot meaning one finger, emerging from a blue sleeve, turning the page of the electronic reader. An historic Quran. I will check the camera later. Ghosts of Marx shaving in the radical bookshop. Waiting and in doing so really feeling like they're really doing something, like, really. Like travelling backwards in time maybe? [Running, alongside the train, a leopard is running.] I will check the camera later. I won’t upload any more photos though due to feeling too conscious of the number already there and knowing that, hey, you’re not my beautiful girlfriend and I’m hopefully not so absurd that I’d ever pretend you were when you weren’t. See the photograph of you stood in front of the huge, painted, blue bird on the wall . . .? Well tomorrow there’ll be a photograph of me stood in a field. So w o ndern o t th en,sov’ reign m i str ess,i fperh aps Th o u c anst[…] D i spl ea sed,S pl endi ddr opl ets ons tri ngs,t h a t I a p p roachthe ethus,importuning vi aSMS, a n d ga z eI nsa tia t e, well [th e h arp ywa s t h etopsthe ysa id] . . . which, in some lights, could be considered possibly a bad thing? The dominance, the authority I mean, the expert status. I will check the camera later. The flash convincing no one the sun is still out. Seeking to travel back to when language began. To convey something specifically British. Which I turn away from for lack of interest. At exactly the same time you turn towards the sculpture and ask ‘what does after mean in that sense as used there?’ After Blake.

Paolozzi. Come on we need to be somewhere that isn't here.

Tracing the roots of a thing – back, to that initial knot of impulses. That bed-sitting room. Via the mean showing).Where was the originary point? Waiting is easy. I am a world champion at it (mis-typed as woCoz what is this other than a text. This is not an experience. It isn't happening). But it is linked. I feel ten influences are not just poetic here, no, my influences include that studio apartment and Ron Silliman I way I go out of my way to imagine reasons for text responses coming, like, 12 hours after the original stuff into this. I enforced a very strict edit . . . & SMS messages are not importuning nowadays nor desig -up grasp of the language game then? *Then that connection between writing better and living happier. .* conversations, well, it was a late late night last night & pages and pages will be deleted soon leaving on every now and again – andis instantly very memorable; kind of. The kind of memory you feel embarraso this so well now. Oh yes then so this shit does bother me believe me. Sorry, of course you believe meneeded as you just have to say believe me and of courseI do and . . . vice-versa. Me and you we say – fu? The person who writes. One gets older and in thatgetting older is a poetry. Each of us returning, one bdid always seem to pass. Because, ultimately, well, not 'ultimately', no (why 'ultimately'?); immediately on the buttons of their phone immediately shouldn't be that surprising should it. . . I mean, there are gam than a conversation. The poetry published by the Cambridge University Press. And, come on, that chick than say. Though re the old days and their institutionalising effects of course I can remember them as I have a so very fascinating. But then the past is a lot like Marbella I hear. And sure, I'll keep hearing that. Expec wooden stool but on a plush dark blue velvet banquette waiting for the play to start. Disembodied, colou grasp of the language game then – . I will post your copy of Beckett's *Trilogy* to you. You left it at my fl Text it. Have those, though, I said. I'm bound to be down again soon, or you up, so why not just hang-on I shouldn't even be talking to you! Some as yet unspecified project is being planned here. Birthday greet ent too early so sent again on the correct day. Accompanied by a poem marking the birthday – this is, yes

this is

this is

this is

this is

this is

this is

this is

this is

this is

this is

this is

this is

this is

this is

this is

this is

this is

this is

this is

this is

this is

this is

this is

This is the train running

The train is running
The train is running

The train is running
This is the train running
The people are going places

Alongside a motorway
, alongside a field

The train is running
The people are going places

Alongside a motorway

He is crossing the field

Whilst the train is running
the train is

also

running

Whilst the train is running
The train is running

Nobody is crying

Walking through the field

When will we get there?

Why are refreshments so dear?

Nobody cries

I just want to get home
now

I should have been home a long time
ago

People are expecting me

Running,
Alongside the train

He is running

He is
, stepping over luggage
Placed unhelpfully in the aisle

Running

Not crying

The train is on time
Passengers waiting for the train
Will not be delayed

The train is on time

, alongside a motorway
, alongside a field

By a wood

He is *crossing* the field

By a wood

He is *by a wood*

He is *crossing the field*
He is *by a wood*

By a wood

He
is
by a wood

A train passes

The people are going
places

He is

By a wood

The Red Rec (Re-Run Channel)

'Talent imitates, genius steals' TS Eliot

'_____________ has moved from presenting children's programmes on the BBC to prime-time family shows on ITV as though there were no difference between the two' A link posted to Marky Bizzle's Facebook profile

Cruel is the new season's schedule
With, in April, the show cancelled
Due to poor feedback returned
By market researchers outside TESCO
ALDI and ASDA asking "the presenters –
Do you find them (a) appealing
(b) unappealing; (c) have no opinion
Or (d) would prefer not to say"
Magazine publication sees: one hell
Of a Twitstorm

& so retreat then to the
Ancestral home: a cramped terrace beside
The out-of-town shopping-centre; we stop in

The food-hall & think about commissioning
editors
The land over; then we talk for an hour
Maybe I should seek new representation
Maybe I shouldn't have so hastily said no to
That 3 page spread in / that magazine, still
Who knew it would end like this
When we were children? He said
This isn't how it ends / Soon a unique and
exciting
Project will emerge just fitted to our talents . . .

We drank coffee then
Read, much of the night
Feeling better, slightly
In the morning

***

What are those roots that clutch, those
branches growing
Preventing you / doing stuff with your
evenings?
You know only images flickering; broken;
pixelated
Beyond recognition / Yet somehow
s o m e h o w

Recognise them you do
Still. Night after night. Your nights
Shattered; re-packaged and sold back to you
In neat little half hour slots
Asking, what next shall we watch?
And not waiting to be answered
The listings internalised
Long ago / The question what's on next
Being rhetorical / You already know what
Is on next / The same that was on last week
and
Two weeks before and the week before that.
This is time devalued – the complete inversion
of time as
'the sphere of human
development'

"Though . . .

Though . . .

Though . . . though . . .

who gives a shit

right?

Really . . .

If this is how we want to spend our lives

who can dis us?

Work is hard and this couch is soft
And this can / this can is cold
But what's inside
Colder still

Forget your rock, red as it might be
I love the cathode ray
And your promise to show something to me
Different to anything I've known previously

my shadow at morning, and
my shadow at evening. Et cetera?

Forget that too"

They gave you anaesthetic first, years ago
They called you the anaesthetised boy
Yet when you came back from surgery, dazed
Begowned: and paper-slippered; you'd lost –

Something. You could not speak / Your eyes
had failed
You were neither living nor dead.

What relaunch possible at 23
Being not even finished properly
In a Version 1 sense then; how to move on to
Version 2? Eh, unwashed unemployed – ?
Civil-servant – ? Supermarket worker – ?
And retired old age pensioner – ? You cannot
say
Or guess, for you know only
Your giro or paltry pay-cheque and so
The question is to you
Akin to asking a cum stain
Why a dead tree gives no shelter
Try though
Or asking the cum stain
Why a dry stone gives no sound of water
Try though

As, these questions are for us now –
These questions –
These questions –
These questions are for us now / all that matter

Show me my image with pink hair, spiked
In your computer; or what I'd look like
With glasses; square; with black plastic frames
Or wearing red trousers

I will show you fear in an office-chair
Punching keys each day for seven hours
                                                  twenty four
For twenty five years for just five days extra
                                                                  leave
That you anyway, when you get it
Don't know what to do with

So never mind your TV career . . .

Snatched away: marking time, instead
Selling gizmos on Free View at 3 AM

Okay, so no one will know who you are?

Mr Ally Ross, very very famous as
Someone who would watch TV
And make vaguely amusing comments
Afterwards, had a bad cold
Nevertheless, his ink ran still
And in his views he concurred

With those market-researched half
To death, in supermarket car-parks
He said things about charisma
Its lack; likeability; intelligence
The absence of that and that and
How mysterious it was
That these idiots had got where they had
Oh Mr Ross . . . Won't you let these innocents
be. . .
If only for one day
Please still your
Vicious tongue
Their careers are short
Though generally their lives
Not so short / Won't you be one of the nice
guys . . .
One has to be so careful these days

Unreal city
City of dreams over the grey fog of
The city of your birth
City to aim for
Take any route necessary there
There's a crowd – see them?
That's where you don't belong
See them queue

For the tram on Friday –
And see them queue for the loo at
The Hungry Horse, every afternoon –
I never thought
Low government investment had
Undone so many, but
I see now that it has, well
Not me

*

A sleeping cat in a pizza box can leave us
Laughing ~~My~~ [our] FAO

after a day on set.

Tweeting pix of the cat we say “London
fashion week starts tomoz –
Shall we go?” Oh *of course we shall go –*
!
And
we shall be on the front row

This is just how we chillax
we think

in a unique way.
Do other's chillax how
we chillax does someone know?

Eh, *do you see? Do you remember?* *Do you know?* I think . . .

Chillaxing is I think

for the birds –
I have never chillaxed in my life ///

/// Now Julie saying "my guess is three" –
meaning when she thinks Bill will be back

from the

pub

Stephen asking (Sarah. Quietly) "so your
husband was painting radiators Saturday at the
post-office?" But asking really "do you think
he's ever been unfaithful to you? Would you

consider infidelity yourself?" And

Pete eating a sandwich
He bought from ALDI; a ploughmans.
When suddenly . . .

Bill is back
Jacket Superdry

Jeans American Apparel
And earlier than expected
Shirt Topman

Bag H+M

Shoes Adidas

Please note: they are steel-capped / The enemy of testicles everywhere

Socks Next

Hat

There wasn't a hat . . .
Lubna says

"Sorry Richard

I have to go and do my prayer". God has written, 'I shall most certainly win, I and my

messengers.' God is powerful and almighty

And we are sure no one ever saw the funny side of cats before us

So when I'm alone / And life is making me lonely, now

I switch on the Radio One breakfast show

*

Today – Now yes I really feel like I have a broader view and more space to be me Nick said

Continuing . . .

And yes, I *have* heard _____ ______ read

What was it like the reading? And the party
after?
Did I know many people?

What with my looking to men of a certain age for hints on masculinity and for tips on how to behave it is no wonder I'm going to have my head done in. And often.

– Avoiding the questions – It is a unique set of circumstances you face every time you open

that door
Some ridiculously glamorous. You might recognise everyone – *Avoiding the questions, still* –
LAST ORDERS HALF PAST TEN
Those Facebook status updates are not true I learnt that for sure. Though that beautiful soul is . . . let's hope it never burns. I thought "good". I was thinking "good", look
Please do not tell me I never tell you what I'm thinking as I just did tell you what I'm thinking
I mean *was* thinking
Then,

just one short moment ago
LAST ORDERS HALF PAST TEN

Now

with Nick back

& Jameela back . . . and it filling up – the flat.
If the Stereophonics have taught us anything –
My eyes don't roll
Why does every
pronouncement have to begin like that?
Where did the analysis
you're choosing annoyingly
To call conversation / where did that come
from? (I knew I shouldn't have waited til
seven
tonight). My flatmate cut himself
shaving. I said, the mere idea of a spa

makes me feel nauseated

A construct
. . . some idea of himself as some kind of
wildman / he is confessional / there is a lack of
control which becomes after a not very short
while

Embarrassing
You have done my head in yes
Yes, let's go – the pub was a bad idea tonight
LAST ORDERS HALF PAST TEN

Though remember, how as a naïve 22 year old
English teacher what you didn't have a clue
about
would have filled the internet – ?
She'll want to know how as a naïve 22 year
old English teacher –
She does. She wants a good time . And if I
don't give it her
With my shooting from the hip and quick
witted banter there's others will, I said

Or he said . . .

Or Nick said . . .

Or Jameela said . . .
LAST ORDERS HALF PAST TEN

LAST ORDERS HALF PAST TEN

LAST ORDERS HALF PAST TEN

In a world where we've never been so well
connected, in truth, we have never been
                    more detached.
Perhaps I should take up tango dancing and
work on my flirty eyes. But the truth is

                                        I can't. That

wouldn't be real.

*

Autumn. And remembering
What was here before
The Trafford Centre was here
And how much better now
The area . . . Run softly home then
Dear shoppers; with your empty bottles
Sandwich papers; silk handkerchiefs
Cardboard boxes; cigarette ends
Et cetera
Yes, they have changed – our addresses
From London's fashionable districts back
To the homes of our parents . . .
Under the Mancunian Way I sat down and
                                                    wept . . .
The rattle of traffic heading . . .

I knew not where
Maybe Ardwick; or
Audenshawe

Unreal city –
Abandoned by the –
Unshaven / and unmade-up
Where is London
When you want London
Eh? Just a train ride away
Just a Virgin Pendolino away
Just a short
    two and half hours away

Which
            at a cost of about £80

      is just too much for me

And
     for
      me
   also
*

Come mid-afternoon we forget, daily

The resilience workshop, where we were
chirpily advised
'When you feel that lull approaching drink
water
Not caffeine. You're just de-hydrated.
Water will see you
right'

Our faces reddening
Our hands warming, holding
Cups of steaming Douwe Egberts, we
Shift positions, stretch our legs
And re-group
round the other side of the desks:

The old man, beady-eyed
Moobs stretching his t-shirt tight, leaning
Leftwards
Due to some kind of infirmity . . . or
Strongly held belief maybe . . . ?

The older man

Younger than the first. Who travelled so far to
be here
And without a day off sick in ten years

Political
Though, just as a corollary of his religious views

The final guest –

The be-gloved lady. Assured as
A Glasgow Contact Centre SEO. Regular achiever of
'The best'; certificates as proof
Herself upholder, also, of an unshakeable faith

Sipping coffee, the three
Skive off
And say

This is wrong and that's wrong –
This needs fixing and that needs fixing –

Continuing
Continuing
Continuing
Con –
To which I respond,
I don't think the problem really is to do with role-models

Rather, a failing
education system unable to
provide the means to allow
people
to make their own
decisions . . .

She turns and looks a moment in her cup
wondering "will my average plus stretch have
been met

tonight by the time I clock out?"
He, unshaven, and with a pocket full of
currants recalls the pleasant whining of the
mandolin
wondering "will I ever hear that music
again and tomorrow will the stationary man –
will he be at
work? – I need envelopes"

Then, having let their colleague's words sink
in . . .

Yes, we agree
X 3

And yes they do.

We agree
We agree
We agree
We agree that (a) education is key; (b)
appearing on TV will not leave a person happy
forever
        and
                anyway
   as an ambition is poor; and
(c) celebrities are not new gods

So we agree, yes
Though interestingly (?) differ in so many
ways

*

Nick Grimshaw, really
What are you doing now?
I am eating toast and drinking
Smoothie, strawberry flavour
Is what you are doing
                        better?

Earlier, I got drunk
I drank 6 cans of beer
The telly was on
I was paying close attention
Now though
My attention
                    it's unfocussed

You're doing s/thing
Pretty glamorous now, right?
Like maybe at a premier
Or interviewing some star
Of Hollyoaks, or whatever

You are bright
And light up the night
Like a flare
Much stronger than candlelight

Nick

Oh Nick
Oh Nick
Oh Nick
Oh Nick

Oh
Nick Grimshaw

*

[poem *for Jameela Jamil*]

This week you notice the girl
On the bus shelter
Though you'd noticed her before
On television
On Sunday, in the morning
advertising a line of clothes
she was promoting
She is very pretty you think
A very pretty, minor celebrity
Her black hair is long
She is long
And she is thin, as well as long
also
Though maybe in the bus-shelter
photo
that longness isn't so noticeable
(Maybe there she's crouching
or something) The girl is
on your mind

during the times when
nothing more important is; ie
on your mind often
And subject of numerous fansites
online, which, this week
you access
via both
your desk top and fone
She is very pretty, yes
She is very pretty

She is very pretty

*

Oh Onan, brother of Er
Brother-in-law of Tamar
If you are called to do your duty
Do it good / And do it proper
Spilled seed
Benefits no one
and will lead to death
Yours, premature. So then forget
Non pro-creative sex (I wrote first
"non *creative* sex" . . .) as
What is it for –

I mean, really
What?

Thinking of foldin' money –
Red, fifties –
Alone in white sterile rooms
They arrive at lonely orgasm

Asking 'what camera is mine?'
And 'is my make-up okay?'
To no one
They cum, alone

In front of TV screens
Lights down, curtains drawn
Prospective lovers passing
Oblivious, outside, they
Cum on their hands to
Celebrity

(Angry at this culture – so impoverished

At success and spending power being forever equated
And failure, failure resulting from

Not wanting things you anyway can't afford
And angry, angry
Yes
At so many people continuing to buy into this . . .

[See, even the language we use –
"buy into this!"]

Seeing a career in the media or TV
As some sort of shortcut to happiness . . .
people with, generally
A great education
Who could be doing something with meaning, choosing instead to
Present links from
One music video to the next music video
et cetera
Coz that's just how much they love cash
Meaning they've fallen for the lies along with the rest of us

And angry at myself too yes of course
For being unable to hate sufficiently some of the people

I feel I really should hate
Due to feeling them just as fucked as I am
And

Angry for being just as thrilled by and in love with
Fun, bright shiny things as
the next person is . . .

I love and am fascinated by this shit, yes.

Though truly hate it
that that's the case)

After the spotlight bright on made-up faces
After the mournful walks through shopping-centres
and such places
After the talks with mum
about living arrangements
Dad silent, impatient
What next eh?
Everyone wants to know
They do; they do; he does; she does; I do
And so do those at home

Those logging onto fan-sites nightly
For news of their favourite celebrity

Here is no applause without cause
Here, no adulation without justification
The road to adulthood runs
Hard and long, but
It's a road that we're all on seeking
Whatever shade we can find

Is time out of work just time to sleep
ready for work again?

Is it healthy to exist just
on the images they feed us
on TV and in the
newspapers?

Are wants the same as needs?

Is it acceptable to receive so many thousands
and thousands of pounds
for reading an Idiot Board
prettily
when so many leave school today
unable to read at all?

Shouldn't we – all of us – be doing a whole lot
more
with our lives?

No

No

No

No

Not in Jerusalem Athens Alexandria
Vienna Manchester or London

No.

None of this is real
Though, someday, real life will begin

'Each individual commodity fights for itself, cannot acknowledge the others and aspires to impose its presence everywhere as though it were alone. The spectacle is the epic poem of this strife – a strife that no fall of Ilium can

bring to an end. Of arms and the man the spectacle does not sing, but rather of passions and the commodity. Within this blind struggle each commodity, following where passion leads, unconsciously actualizes something of a higher order than itself: the commodity's becoming worldly coincides with the world's being transformed into commodities . . . ' Guy Debord, The Society of the Spectacle

***

A woman draws her long black hair out tight
And updates her Tumblr
With a link to a cat walking upright
Before falling over / She captions it
LOL
And
Yes, she is laughing
She is laughing because she is happy
(So that's okay)

A man crawls head downward down a blackened wall
Tweeting / on his way
'OMG Lindsey Lohan and Branson

In space / I heard today!'
LOL (again)
And yes he is laughing
He is laughing, really
He is laughing because he is happy
(So that's okay)

The good old days when breathing in was something you only needed to do under water / Everything I like is either illegal; immoral; fattening; addictive; expensive; or impossible / You fed me truth from a half-baked lie / Sex is like pizza: when it's good it's good and when it's bad it's still pretty good / I'm sorry I sharpened the thorn in your side/ I was standing there in some sort of hazy stupor, breathless and weighed down / There is nothing more I DARE ask out of life . . .

We are happy as, today
Contracts were signed
And exchanged

*

Mon 5th November. 20.00.
New series. ____ ________ and _______ _____ get their clothes muddy racing high-powered quad bikes around the Welsh countryside and then find out if a hi-tech washer-dryer can get them clean again. In the Porth yr Ogof caves near the Brecon Beacons they explore the pitch-black labyrinth of rivers and passageways to test the quality of torch batteries, and at St Donat's castle they listen to a performance by Only Boys Aloud to review a set of in-ear headphones. The pair also have fun with a karaoke app and an electronic musical instrument, try out three entry-level smartphones and send tiny HD cameras up in a weather balloon to film the stratosphere

Notes

‘The Red Rec (Re-Run Channel)’ is an over-writing and updating of ‘The Wasteland’. As such, within the text several word-clusters and line-fragments from that earlier poem remain intact. The other sources drawn upon, both credited in the text and not, are Guy Debord’s *The Society of The Spectacle*; The Sun newspaper; the Tumblr, Twitter feed, bus-shelter clothes adverts and online *Company* magazine columns of Jameela Jamil. *The Qur’an* (M. A. S. Abdel Haleem translation); *Downtown* (Petula Clark version; composed by Tony Hatch); *Hairdresser on Fire* (Morrissey); the ’Onan’ Wikipedia page; and The Daily Star online.

The poem is for PM; BS; JD; LH; GM and SV.

Penniless Poetix

1#

Long months spent measuring the distance between points. Recognising link-ups occur only between pairs with all contrary claims now discarded. I will leave soon he said. I will leave that anaemic account behind as tomorrow theft will be legalised. These things need doing urgently – saying we inhabit a web-like structure and that connections are fluid is just a dodge to avoid doing them. Everyone is so career oriented – me included. My latest research has been deemed unpublishable - they asked “who wants to know that the stars link up only in twos?” Who could be surprised that after being told forever “you need this thing yet we will keep from you the means of getting it” one day they decided to just take the thing for themselves? This came as no shock to me. His refusal to bow to far left pressure, going so far as to call the police, absolutely did though (yet only heightened my admiration for him) – theft being now personal in the same way the political is you see. So I am now vaccinated against rhizomatic virus. The first few days were hard but I'm getting better, slowly. Unhappy about the refusal to condemn, therefore that itself being condemned. What is writing? What use is writing today? Sat here comfortably dreaming of drinking the blood of David Cameron and pitying a, in comparison, safe safe text. You say "I will book the Travel Lodge for the end of January. Everything will be okay".

2#

The dilemma was to do with use diminishing the critical distance (a conference of legitimacy upon abhorrent views?) But it was the wrong dilemma. Tired of using the line about domestic circumstances being complicated boiling down to a long succession of nights spent lonely at home. If you want it then (and you do. The message being perfect) / Take it, the voice said. Overwrite it and/or update it and/or significantly borrow from it – . My pissy liberal conscience makes me sick. Knowing the end point always to be the turning into style – I mean, no matter how far we go we can't return to the beginning and style to revolt – it was perhaps more than stupid of him then to attempt to do exactly that.

The Bang & Olufsen catalogue, summer 2011

The JD Sports catalogue, summer 2011

LateRooms.com, today

In retrospect it seemed fresher source material was called for

Bonney showed (as he has showed again and again and will continue to do so).

No one will be offended. Do not worry. Please

3# *(New Year's Eve. 2017)*

Do you remember how easy laughter came back then? How necessary it was?

4#

Dead men and women paraded before us as we parade before them, dead ourselves. The laughter of the last people on earth. The possibility of a transcendental criticism well and truly demolished now. This stink is beautiful. This earth beneath my feet is beautiful. How easy it is to forget though night after night spent laughing and laughing and laughing and – and not having an answer when asked why you are laughing. Tomorrow the gates will be rolled back. Jails rebranded as desirable starter homes with good transport links for, um – . And we will never go back there. The constellations are lies. Yes, dreams are haunted by all that wasn't done and was caused not to be done. Only twos twos twos and twos. And yes, a multiplicity but of just things and their opposites (it must be so otherwise how could progress be possible?). They wanted things so they just took them. Which is the fault only of ruling class ideology (and contributory factor to its eventual downfall) – how this country turns rain into something that doesn't feel like rain, smell like rain or even look like water. Has anyone ever lost their life due to infringement of intellectual copyright? Is a very very funny question –

HA HA HA!

HA HA HA!

HA HA

HA!

HA HA HA!

Oh how we love to laugh –

Yes, at the TV we watch

At the poems we read

At ourselves

And at each other

(Somewhere in the world right now a TV personality is receiving or performing oral sex

While in the back room of a house in Salford a poet is thinking about how

Somewhere in the world right now a TV personality is receiving or performing oral sex

And typing onto their Word document the sentence

Somewhere in the world right now a TV personality is receiving or performing oral sex

A sentence you have just read)

*

Salford: 2008. Documenting the collapse of Lehman Brothers. Sean Bonney's The Commons

Moston : 2009. Domestic retreat
Manchester: Summer, 2011. Riots break out across the UK. Deleuze and Guattari's A Thousand

Plateaus
Cambridge, London, Manchester: 2012 – . Ariana Reines' Coeur de Lion. Theodor Adorno's Minima

Moralia

Rediscovery of the dialectic

Plus, the bleed through, in both directions, between society and art

5#

Triangulate consumer, producer and poet. It being ridiculous to think of that last as being un-implicated – . Then listen to the conversation "it's hard for me you know knowing you go home to him every night while I am alone". The dialectic differs from the argument in the latter always implying a victor. Hear them say then we are all of us in the shit. Specifically "do you not think it's hard for me as well?" Inspiration is a myth. As a poet you are not more sensitive, clever or observant than a non-poet. You are just someone who reads and writes poetry. Take feedback on board. I shouldn't phone when drunk. Do not phone me when drunk. Likewise, off-hand references to TS Eliot may just result in something interesting. I cannot be angry at someone suffering from what I have I say, can I – with, tomorrow, every single jail cell empty - this laziness and addiction to all that is bright, diverting and fun . . .

But you’re leaving. Your research here done.
I think you heard.

Bibliography

Cited Works

Adorno, Theodor. *Minima Moralia*. London & New York: Verso Books, 1993.

Bonney, Sean. *The Commons*. London: Openned Press, 2011.

Deleuze, Gilles and Guattari, Felix. *A Thousand Plateaus*. London: Continuum, 2004.

Reines, Ariana. *Coeur de Lion*. Albany, NY: Fence Books, 2011.

Consulted Works

Bonney, Sean '*after Rimbaud: The Kidnap and Murder of David Cameron*'. abandonedbuildings.blogspot.co.uk/2012/12/after-rimbaud-kidnap-and-murder-of.html Web : 10/12/12.

Bonney, Sean. *Document*. London: Barque Press, 2009.

Hayward, Danny. *RIOT POLIT-ECON: A Joint Report of the Khalid Qureshi Foundation and the Chelsea Ives Youth Centre* (Publication details unknown. Circulated via email by the Miami University, UK poetry list on 13 July 2012).

Hind, Colleen & Mildew, Pocahontas. *We Are Real: A History.* Cambridge: Critical Documents, 2012.

Home, Stewart. *The Assault on Culture*. London & Edinburgh: AK Press, 1991.

Home, Stewart. *Neoist Manifestoes / The Art Strike Papers*. London & Edinburgh: AK Press, 1991.

Home, Stewart. *Neoism Plagiarism & Praxis*. London & Edinburgh: AK Press, 1995.

Horkheimer, Max and Adorno, Theodor. 'Elements of Anti-Semitism: Limits of Enlightenment' from *Dialectic of Enlightenment*. New York: Continuum, 2001.

Melly, George. *Revolt into Style*. London: Faber and Faber, 2009.

Seale, Bobby. *Seize the Time: The Story of the Black Panther Party*. London: Arrow Books, 1970.

Thomson, Alex. *Adorno: A Guide for the Perplexed*. London: Continuum, 2006.

Watson, Ben. *Adorno for Revolutionaries*. London: Unkant, 2011.

Watson, Ben. *Art, Class & Cleavage*. London: Quartet Book: 1998.

www.ingramcontent.com/pod-product-compliance
Ingram Content Group UK Ltd.
Pitfield, Milton Keynes, MK11 3LW, UK
UKHW020220250726
13967UKWH00001B/96

9 781291 544978